Sparrows & Finches

OF THE GREAT LAKES REGION & EASTERN NORTH AMERICA

Chris G. Earley

FIREFLY BOOKS

A FIREFLY BOOK

Published by Firefly Books Ltd. 2003

First Printing 2003

U.S. Cataloging-in-Publication Data (Library of Congress standards)

Earley, Chris.
    Sparrows and Finches of the Great Lakes Region and Eastern North America / Chris Earley. – 1st ed.
[128] p. : ill. : col. photos, maps ; cm.
Includes bibliographical references and index.
Summary: A field guide to 60 sparrows and finches including 200 color photographs, detailed descriptions of song, habitat and plumage changes according to season and gender.
ISBN 1-55297-707-2 (pbk.)
ISBN 1-55297-804-4

1. Sparrows – East (U.S.) – Identification.
2. Sparrows – Lake States – Identification.
3. Sparrows – Canada, Eastern – Identification.
1. Finches – East (U.S.) – Identification.
2. Finches – Lake States – Identification.
3. Finches – Canada, Eastern – Identification.
I. Title.

598.8/ 83/ 097 21   QL696.P2438.E17   2003

National Library of Canada Cataloguing in Publication Data

Earley, Chris G., 1968-
    Sparrows and Finches of the Great Lakes Region and Eastern North America / Chris Earley.
Includes bibliographical references and index.
ISBN 1-55297-707-2 (pbk.)
ISBN 1-55297-804-4 (bound)

1. Sparrows – Great Lakes Region – Identification.
2. Sparrows – Canada, Eastern – Identification.
3. Sparrows – East (U.S.) – Identification.
4. Finches – Great Lakes Region – Identification.
5. Finches – Canada, Eastern – Identification.
6. Finches – East (U.S.) – Identification. I. Title.

QL696.P2E277 2003   598.8'83'09713
C2002-905404-4

Published in the U.S. in 2003 by
Firefly Books (U.S.) Inc.
P.O. Box 1338, Ellicott Station
Buffalo, New York 14205

Design by Lind Design
Printed and bound in Singapore
by Tien Wah Press (Pte) Ltd

Published in Canada in 2003 by
Firefly Books Ltd.
3680 Victoria Park Avenue
Toronto, Ontario M2H 3K1

The Publisher acknowledges the financial support of the Government of Canada through the Book Publishing Industry Development Program for its publishing activities.

Front cover photo: McCaw
Back cover photo: Small

Table of Contents

LBJs and you

With practice, persistence, and above all, patience, you will soon be able to identify sparrows.

THOSE LBJs (LITTLE BROWN JOBS)! "THEY ALL LOOK the same to me" seems to be a common statement from many beginning birders. And they do all look the same – at first. With practice, persistence, and above all, patience, you will soon be able to identify sparrows and other birds with cone-shaped beaks, such as finches and buntings.

When trying to identify birds it is important to remember the following motto: *I don't know.*

Really, it's okay to say it. Too many birders will get an inconclusive view of a bird and then just guess. With practice, you can identify birds from incredibly short glimpses of them, but there will always be some "I don't knows." And even if you do get a good look and still can't identify the bird, you will have learned from the process. The next time you see that species, it will be familiar to you and you may see another field mark or behavior to help in its identification. And don't forget to watch the birds as well! Keeping a checklist is fun and a way to record your sightings, but careful observations will help you really understand these interesting creatures. Watching birds in their environment reveals interactions that link all of nature together.

MCCAW

How to use this book (terminology)

♂ = MALE   **♀ = FEMALE**

If there is no symbol, then the male/female plumage is not significantly different.

SUMMER Spring and summer months' plumage.

WINTER Autumn and winter months' plumage.

ADULT Birds that are over one year old (i.e., not in their first winter or first summer plumage). If there is no distinctive winter or summer plumage, then the entry will say only "adult."

FIRST WINTER Some birds have a distinctive plumage during their first autumn and winter.

FIRST SUMMER Some birds have a distinctive plumage in the first full spring and summer after they hatch.

JUVENILE Most small birds have a distinctive juvenile plumage when they leave the nest, but because this lasts for only a very short time, it is not represented in this book. The juvenile plumages of a few very common backyard species are shown.

LISTEN FOR Learning and remembering sparrow and finch songs are very important skills to help you locate and identify the shyer species. The most common song used by each species is given *in blue italics*. Most small birds also have distinctive non-song sounds (calls) that can be heard as they forage or scold potential predators. Utilize other bird books for more examples of songs and calls. There are many great bird recordings that can help show the differences between species. Once you know a few of the songs you will be surprised at how many more sparrows and finches you'll see because you heard them first.

COMPARE TO This lists other birds that look similar to this particular sparrow or finch. At the back of the book you will find comparison pages. These will be helpful for comparing similar species.

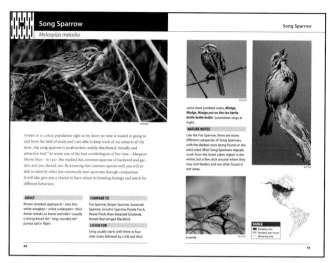

The box at the top left of the page graphically represents the adult female's breast pattern and color to help beginners differentiate between birds with similar patterns.

SEASONAL STATUS

This list (pages 14–15) refers to the seasonal status of sparrows and finches at Point Pelee National Park. Because Point Pelee is a central point for much of the Great Lakes region, you can use this information as a guideline for when these birds may arrive or leave your area. For example, Point Pelee is at roughly the same latitude as Chicago and the northern border between Pennsylvania and New York state, so seasonal status in these areas may be similar. As another example, consider that the average spring first-arrival date of a migratory species at Point Pelee likely precedes the first-arrival date of that species in more northerly Milwaukee or Toronto by about four to six days.

RANGE MAPS

These maps show each species' breeding and wintering ranges, as well as where they may be resident all year long.

A note to beginners

Don't just learn their markings, but learn their shapes and flight patterns, too.

WHEN LOOKING AT sparrows and finches, resist the urge to instantly start flipping through this guide. Watch the bird first. This way you can look for field marks and behaviors before the bird disappears from your view. Ask yourself questions such as:

"What markings does it have on its breast? Does it have wing-bars, an eyering, an eyebrow? Does it have a long or short tail? What does it sound like?"

After answering these and other questions, *then* look in this book. Sparrows can be very shy and hard to find in the underbrush, and you should spend your time looking at them before they move on.

Try to learn the common species of your area first. Don't just learn their markings, but learn their shapes and flight patterns, too. Being familiar with shape, size, behavior and movements of common sparrows and finches will help with identification of the less common or migratory species that you will come across.

The quotes

MANY OF THE descriptions in this book include a quote from naturalist writings on bird behavior and identification. While these observations may seem unscientific or "fluffy" to many readers, I believe that these naturalists have a magnificent understanding of birds and their lives. While giving non-human creatures human characteristics (anthropomorphism) is unscientific, I believe that beginners can benefit from this practice. What better way for a human to initially learn about something than to use human-like descriptions? So try reading the quotes, then watch a sparrow feeding or listen to a finch singing. You may find that the melodramatic or colorful style does indeed apply to your subject. If you still find the quotes aren't for you, just skip them and use the other information. There are many different learning styles.

While giving non-human creatures human characteristics is unscientific, beginners can benefit from this practice.

Taxonomy

Many different bird groups have adapted to eating seeds—and they have the cone-shaped beaks to prove it.

NOT ALL "SPARROWS" end up being sparrows. Especially for beginners, distinguishing a sparrow from a finch is difficult. That is why this book includes finches as well as buntings, grosbeaks and other birds with cone-shaped beaks. And because many finch species come to bird feeders in the winter, many birders will be seeing these birds in their own backyards—a perfect time to practice identification skills.

Many of the birds described here are not even closely related to each other (see next page). Most of the sparrows are actually more closely related to warblers and tanagers than to the finches. This may seem confusing, but just keep in mind that there are many different bird groups that have adapted to eating seeds—and they have the cone-shaped beaks to prove it.

The order of the birds in this book follows the seventh edition of the American Ornithologists' Union Check-list of North American Birds, 1998. The birds are arranged in a specific sequence (taxonomic order) that recognizes relationships between species. You may notice that many closely related birds, such as the *Spizella* sparrows, will have similar behaviors, shapes and bill sizes. This will hopefully help you to use shape and behavior as identification aids as well as to learn a bit about taxonomic relationships among birds.

Classification of the birds in this book

HERE IS A LIST that shows how the birds in this book are classified. Each genus in a family is listed to show which species are closely related.

Class Aves: Birds
Order Passeriformes: Passerine or perching birds

FAMILY EMBERIZIDAE: EMBERIZIDS

Genus		
	Pipilo	towhees
	Spizella	American Tree, Clay-colored, Chipping, Field Sparrow
	Pooecetes	Vesper Sparrow
	Chondestes	Lark Sparrow
	Passerculus	Savannah Sparrow
	Ammodramus	Grasshopper, Henslow's, Le Conte's, Nelson's Sharp-tailed, Seaside
	Passerella	Fox Sparrow
	Melospiza	Song, Lincoln's, Swamp Sparrow
	Zonotrichia	White-throated, Harris's, White-crowned Sparrow
	Junco	Dark-eyed Junco
	Calcarius	longspurs
	Plectrophenax	Snow Bunting

FAMILY CARDINALIDAE: CARDINALS AND ALLIES

Genus		
	Cardinalis	Northern Cardinal
	Pheucticus	Rose-breasted Grosbeak
	Passerina	Blue Grosbeak, Indigo Bunting
	Spiza	Dickcissel

FAMILY FRINGILLIDAE: FRINGILLINE OR WINTER FINCHES

Genus		
	Pinicola	Pine Grosbeak
	Carpodacus	Purple, House Finch
	Loxia	crossbills
	Carduelis	redpolls, siskin, goldfinch
	Coccothraustes	Evening Grosbeak

FAMILY PASSERIDAE: OLD WORLD SPARROWS

Genus		
	Passer	House Sparrow

Identification features

Rump Back Eyebrow Central crown stripe Lateral crown stripe Lore

White-throated Sparrow

Wingbars Eyeline Throat

Cheek Eyering Crown

Vesper Sparrow

Undertail coverts Flank Belly Breast

Sparrow & finch look-alikes

FIGURING OUT WHICH birds are sparrows and finches and which aren't can be confusing because of similarities in a few other bird groups. For example, some female blackbirds can look surprisingly like some of the sparrows, but they tend to be much bigger and have a different overall shape. Taking the time to study these birds when you see them will help you with future sparrow identifications.

The female Bobolink looks like many sparrows but is buffier overall. It is in the blackbird family.

The female Red-winged Blackbird is similar to some female finches and the female Rose-breasted Grosbeak, but it has a longer beak and a longer tail.

The female Brown-headed Cowbird looks surprisingly similar to the female Indigo Bunting, but it is bigger and has a heavier-looking beak.

Another look-alike is the American Pipit, but watch for its narrow, thin beak.

Seasonal status of sparrows & finches
for Point Pelee National Park

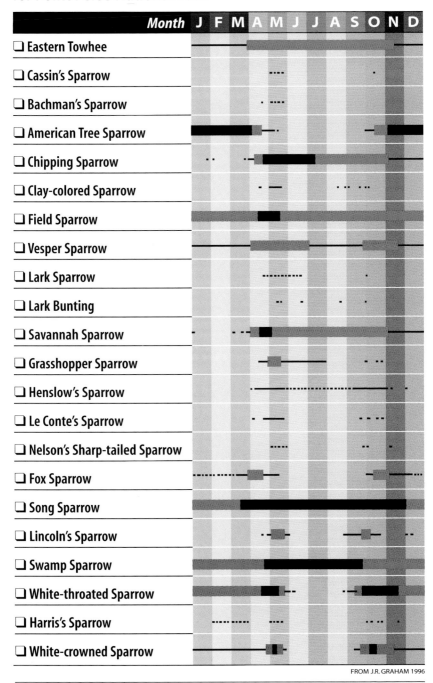

Month	J	F	M	A	M	J	J	A	S	O	N	D
❑ Eastern Towhee												
❑ Cassin's Sparrow												
❑ Bachman's Sparrow												
❑ American Tree Sparrow												
❑ Chipping Sparrow												
❑ Clay-colored Sparrow												
❑ Field Sparrow												
❑ Vesper Sparrow												
❑ Lark Sparrow												
❑ Lark Bunting												
❑ Savannah Sparrow												
❑ Grasshopper Sparrow												
❑ Henslow's Sparrow												
❑ Le Conte's Sparrow												
❑ Nelson's Sharp-tailed Sparrow												
❑ Fox Sparrow												
❑ Song Sparrow												
❑ Lincoln's Sparrow												
❑ Swamp Sparrow												
❑ White-throated Sparrow												
❑ Harris's Sparrow												
❑ White-crowned Sparrow												

FROM J.R. GRAHAM 1996

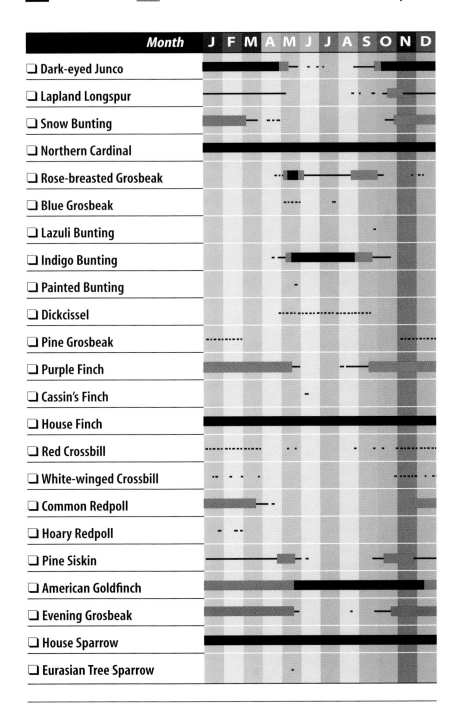

Month	J	F	M	A	M	J	J	A	S	O	N	D
❑ Dark-eyed Junco												
❑ Lapland Longspur												
❑ Snow Bunting												
❑ Northern Cardinal												
❑ Rose-breasted Grosbeak												
❑ Blue Grosbeak												
❑ Lazuli Bunting												
❑ Indigo Bunting												
❑ Painted Bunting												
❑ Dickcissel												
❑ Pine Grosbeak												
❑ Purple Finch												
❑ Cassin's Finch												
❑ House Finch												
❑ Red Crossbill												
❑ White-winged Crossbill												
❑ Common Redpoll												
❑ Hoary Redpoll												
❑ Pine Siskin												
❑ American Goldfinch												
❑ Evening Grosbeak												
❑ House Sparrow												
❑ Eurasian Tree Sparrow												

Legend: ■ Common   ■ Uncommon   —— Rare   ----- Very Rare

Pipilo erythrophthalmus

Male

"I HEARD A CLAMOR in the underbrush beside me, a rustle of an animal's approach. It sounded as though the animal was about the size of a bobcat, a small bear, or a large snake. The commotion stopped and started, coming ever nearer. The agent of all this ruckus proved to be, of course, a towhee." (Annie Dillard, *Pilgrim at Tinker Creek*, 1974). What naturalist hasn't been surprised by the amount of noise that a small bird such as a towhee can make? These ground-dwelling birds are notorious for scratching loudly in the leaf litter, but can be quite difficult to see. Fortunately they have a very distinctive song.

♂ ADULT

A very large sparrow (cardinal-size)
• long tail • *black head and breast*
• black upperparts • white wing patches
• white corners and sides of tail • *rufous sides* • white belly.

♀ ADULT

Same as male but *brown replacing black*.

LISTEN FOR

The song is a variable *drink your teeeeeee* with the "tea" part being a musical trill. The call is *to-whee* or *che-wink* or *joree*, all of which have at one time been this bird's common name.

COMPARE TO

See its western counterpart, the Spotted Towhee, in the Vagrant section (page 99).

Female

NATURE NOTES

This species is such a vigorous singer that it has even been known to sing when it is held for banding. One adventurous towhee was found in England in 1966. This species was once called the "Rufous-sided Towhee" (which is much more fun to say than its current name).

Male

RANGE

- Breeding only
- Resident year round
- Wintering only

Spizella arborea

Adult

WHILE THIS SPARROW breeds in the very far north of North America, it is a common visitor to many Great Lakes region bird feeders in winter. It often searches the ground under feeders along with Dark-eyed Juncos, preferring millet over most other seeds. The American Tree Sparrow is a fairly easy sparrow to identify, as its bicolored beak and unstreaked breast with a central spot is a distinctive combination. For a week or two in April, its look-alike, the Chipping Sparrow, may share the bird feeder – a good chance for you to do some comparisons (see comparison pages 114–115).

ADULT

Rufous crown • grey head • *rufous eyeline* • *bicolored beak* • greyish-white underparts • *central breast spot* • white wingbars • streaked back • rufous wash on sides.

LISTEN FOR

The song of the American Tree Sparrow can sometimes be heard in late winter/ early spring before the birds start heading north. It is a clear, whistled, musical warble described by Thoreau as *"twitter twitter twe twe twe."* He goes on to describe the call of this sparrow as sounding like the tinkling of an icicle. I like to think they are saying a cheerful, jingling *we-will-eat* as they zip around the winter feeder.

This individual has a less distinctive central breast spot.

REAUME

COMPARE TO

Field Sparrow, Chipping Sparrow, Swamp Sparrow and Lark Sparrow (see comparison pages 114–115).

NATURE NOTES

American Tree Sparrows have been known to roost under the snow's surface. These sparrows often line their nests with ptarmigan feathers. After an October storm in 1907, W.E. Saunders counted 358 dead American Tree Sparrows in three hours while walking along a Lake Huron beach.

RANGE

- ■ Breeding only
- ☐ Wintering only

Spizella passerina

Summer Adult

THIS IS A COMMON suburban sparrow of summer. It often nests in the Colorado Blue Spruce in the front yard, giving observers a great chance to watch its breeding cycle. The easiest way to find a nest is to watch for a female collecting nesting material. But you have only a small window of opportunity, as it takes her just four days to build the nest. The winter plumage of the Chipping Sparrow can be seen in the fall, but very few stay in the Great Lakes region for the winter.

SUMMER ADULT

Reddish cap • *white eyebrow* • black eyeline • *dark beak* • grey nape • streaked brown upperparts • *grey rump* • white wingbars • whitish throat and undertail coverts • grey underparts.

WINTER ADULT

Similar to summer except • brownish cap • buffy eyebrow • *pinkish beak* • brownish wash to flanks • (First winter similar but a bit buffier overall and may have a brownish rump.)

Winter   MCCAW

Winter: The grey rump is usually present in all plumages.

Juvenile: Note that this plumage has distinctive breast streaks.

COMPARE TO

Field and Swamp Sparrows in summer, Clay-colored Sparrow, American Tree Sparrow and female House Sparrow in fall (see comparison pages 114–115).

LISTEN FOR

A long, unmusical trill, usually on one pitch, but some may have a slight variation. May sing at night.

NATURE NOTES

This species has likely benefited from the clearing of forests and spread of human habitation. It was once called the "Horsehair Bird" because it lined its nest with horse-hair. Now it tends to use dog, cattle, deer, raccoon or even human hair instead.

RANGE
- Breeding only
- Resident year round
- Wintering only

Spizella pallida

Summer adult
FLYNN

THE CLAY-COLORED SPARROW is at its easternmost range in the Great Lakes region. Root (in Bent, 1968) describes it as "a trim little fellow, neat of form, clothed in mostly shades of brown and gray, with clay-colored trimmings and a three-cornered ear patch of darker brown. A gray and buffy streaked crown helps to distinguish him from his city cousin, the Chipping Sparrow." The song of the Clay-colored Sparrow is quite distinctive. One habitat to listen for it is in an open field scattered with young spruce trees.

SUMMER ADULT

Brown streaked cap with a white central crown stripe • white eyebrow • pinkish beak • *dark-bordered, buffy cheek patch* • white wingbars • brown streaked back • buffy-brown rump • grey underparts.

WINTER ADULT

Similar to summer except • less distinctive head markings • a buffy wash on breast, sides and eyebrow • (First winter similar but may be buffier.)

COMPARE TO

Chipping Sparrow in fall. Note that fall Clay-coloreds have light lores and brownish rumps and Chipping Sparrows have dark lores and (usually) grey rumps.

LISTEN FOR

A very insect-like ***buzz buzz buzz***.

Summer adult

MCCAW

NATURE NOTES

The Clay-colored Sparrow was first collected in Saskatchewan by Richardson and Drummond, the naturalists who accompanied Sir John Franklin on his land-based Arctic expeditions.

Summer adult

MCCAW

RANGE

■ Breeding only
  Wintering only

Spizella pusilla

Adult

THE UNIQUE SONG of the Field Sparrow makes it one of the most easily learned bird songs. Thoreau (1851) wrote that this species "jingles her small change, pure silver, on the counter of the pasture," an accurate description of this bird's accelerating whistles. It often sings all day long, even in the afternoon. Samuels (in Studer, 1881) wrote, "Mounted on a low tree or fence-rail, he utters his pleasing, yet plaintive ditty at early morning and evening, and, in dark and cloudy weather, through the whole day." I've heard them sing in the middle of the night as well.

ADULT

Grey head • *rufous cap* • *rufous eyeline* • *pink beak* • *white eyering* (sometimes hard to see) • brown streaked upperparts • *grey rump* • white wingbars • greyish underparts • rufous wash on sides.

LISTEN FOR

A series of accelerating, clear whistles that rises in pitch. Its pattern gives the impression of a bouncing ping-pong ball. May sing at night.

COMPARE TO

Chipping Sparrow, American Tree Sparrow, Swamp Sparrow, first winter White-crowned Sparrow (see comparison pages 114–115).

Adult

MCCAW

NATURE NOTES

There is a record of this sparrow nesting within 45 cm of an Eastern Towhee nest. After feeding their own young, each species would then feed the other's nestlings! It is sometimes found at Great Lakes region feeders in winter, so learn to distinguish the Field Sparrow from the more common wintering American Tree Sparrow (see comparison pages 114–115). Many species of snakes, such as blue racers, milk snakes, rattlesnakes and garter snakes are known to eat eggs and/or nestling Field Sparrows. Adult field sparrows may pretend to have a broken wing to lead predators away from fledglings.

MCCAW

This summer individual shows how worn its plumage can look before it molts.

RANGE

■	Breeding only
■	Resident year round
■	Wintering only

Pooecetes gramineus

Adult

"THE WHITE-IN-TAILS, or grass finches, linger pretty late…but they come so near winter only as the white in their tail indicates. They let it come near enough to whiten their tails, perchance, and they are off." So writes Thoreau in 1854 about the Vesper Sparrow. This streaked sparrow does have distinctive white outer tail feathers, but as these aren't always seen, it is best to learn its facial pattern for identification purposes. As Thoreau states, most are gone for the winter, but a few are reported in the Great Lakes region all year long. When here in the summer, the Vesper Sparrow can be found if you "go to those broad, smooth, up-lying fields where the cattle and sheep are grazing, and sit down on one of the warm, clean stones, and listen to this song…such an unambitious, unconscious melody! It is one of the most characteristic sounds of nature." (John Burroughs in Studer, 1881)

This individual shows a central breast spot.

Note chestnut shoulder.

ADULT

Dark bordered cheek patch • thin white eyering • streaked brown above • chestnut shoulder patch (often concealed) *• fine dark streaks on white or buffy breast • sometimes a central breast spot • white outer tail feathers.*

COMPARE TO

Song, Savannah, Lincoln's, winter Lapland Longspur, American Pipit.

LISTEN FOR

Song is similar to the Song Sparrow's, but a bit more musical and starting with two pairs of notes. Thoreau described it as, **"here here there there quick quick quick or I'm gone."** The name Vesper comes from the fact that this bird often sings in the evening time, but it is a a misnomer as it also sings during the day and sometimes at night.

NATURE NOTES

Besides the names given above, this sparrow was once called the Bay-winged Bunting, because of its chestnut shoulder patches. It is often found in the cultivated fields of agricultural areas.

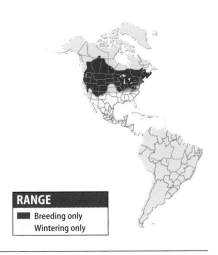

RANGE	
■	Breeding only
	Wintering only

Chondestes grammacus

Adult

SMALL

THIS IS ONE of the most striking of our sparrows with its boldly patterned head of rufous, black and white. "When pairing season commences, the males are very pugnacious, fighting often on the wing, and the conquering rival repairing to the nearest bush, tunes his lively pipe in token of success. They sing sweetly, and, like the Larks, have the habit of continuing their notes while on the wing." (Studer, 1881)

ADULT

Rufous crown, white central crown stripe, white eyebrow, black eyeline, *rufous cheek bordered with white and black,* greyish beak that is paler below, grey nape, brown upperparts with dark streaks on back, white to dull white underparts, *central breast spot,* light brown wash on flanks, white tipped tail feathers and white outer tail feathers.

FIRST WINTER

Similar to adult but duller overall with little or no rufous color in cap or cheek. Some streaks on breast and flanks.

COMPARE TO

American Tree Sparrow.

LISTEN FOR

A variable series of clear whistles, buzzier notes and trills.

Lark Sparrow

Note central breast spot. MCCAW

Note white tipped tail. SMALL

First winter MCCAW

NATURE NOTES

This western species spread eastward as forests were cleared. Its number's have dropped here recently, likely due to the resurgence of second-growth forest.

RANGE

- Breeding only
- Resident year round
- Wintering only

Adult

FAIRBAIRN

THESE PERKY LITTLE sparrows are frequent finds in open habitats across the Great Lakes region – their breeding range covers the whole area and extends to the subarctic shores of Hudson Bay. Distinguishing Song and Savannah Sparrows is one of the first big challenges that beginning birders have. Shape is an important feature, as the Savannah Sparrow has a fairly short, notched tail in comparison to the long, rounded tail of the Song Sparrow. The yellow lores of the Savannah Sparrow are another distinctive feature, but are not always present.

ADULT

Often yellowish lores • white central crown stripe • brown streaked above • white underparts • fine dark breast streaks • often a central breast spot • *shortish, notched tail*.

COMPARE TO

Song, Vesper and Lincoln's as well as American Pipit.

LISTEN FOR

A song that starts jumbled and then ends buzzy. I always think they are singing, *"won't you sit down besiiiiiiiiiiiiiide meee?"*

Adult   MCCAW

Adult   MCCAW

NATURE NOTES

Clapper Rails are known to eat adults during migration and on breeding grounds. Though the name "Savannah" fits the habitat preferences of this sparrow, it was actually named by Alexander Wilson for the place that the first described specimen was collected – Savannah, Georgia.

RANGE

- Breeding only
- Resident year round
- Wintering only

Ammodramus savannarum

Adult

THIS SPECIES IS A good example of why knowing a bird's song is very important. Grasshopper Sparrows can be quite shy, so listening for them is definitely the way to find one. But be warned, the song is so insect-like that you really should listen to a tape to know what they sound like first. It may seem like a lot of trouble now, but finding one of these little guys singing from the top of a small shrub in a dry open area is worth the effort.

ADULT

Fairly large beak • flat head • thin whitish eyering • buffy face with a dark spot behind eye • orangish lores • dark cap with a whitish central stripe • gray nape with thin rusty streaks • yellow can sometimes be seen on the bend of the folded wing • buffy breast • whitish belly • short tail.

COMPARE TO

Le Conte's Sparrow (see *Ammodramus* comparison pages 116–117).

LISTEN FOR

A couple of quiet, short chip notes followed by an insect-like buzz.

NATURE NOTES

The yellow in the wing once earned this species the name "Yellow-winged Bunting." When disturbed, it often runs along the ground, mouse-like, instead of flying.

This individual shows the yellow in the bend of the wing.

SMALL

Adult

MCCAW

Adil

MCCAW

Adult

RANGE
- Breeding only
- Resident year round
- Wintering only

Ammodramus henslowii

Adult   FLYNN

IN 1934, ROGER TORY PETERSON described the Henslow's Sparrow's song as "one of the poorest vocal efforts of any bird, a hiccoughing 'tsi-lick'." But this song is likely the only way that you'll know if a Henslow's Sparrow is on a breeding territory. Its secretive habits and reluctance to fly keep it hidden from most observers. This species is declining in numbers throughout the region.

ADULT

Large beak • *olive-green face* • buffy central crown stripe • brown streaked above • *rufous in wings* • buffy breast • *narrow dark streaks on breast and sides* • whitish belly • pointed tail feathers.

COMPARE TO

Le Conte's Sparrow (see *Ammodramus* comparison pages 116–117).

LISTEN FOR

An dry, short, insect-like *"tsi-lick."*

NATURE NOTES

One survey method that researchers use for finding Henslow's Sparrows is to listen in the correct habitat in the middle of the night, a common time for this bird to sing.

Adult   FLYNN

Adult   FLYNN

RANGE
Breeding only
Wintering only

Ammodramus leconteii

Adult

FLYNN

ANOTHER SECRETIVE *Ammodramus* sparrow, the Le Conte's Sparrow was first described in 1790, then not described again until 1843. Then the third specimen was taken in 1872. Obviously a hard bird to study! Both this and the Henslow's Sparrow were once called "stink birds" because hunting dogs would often point to them instead of quail.

ADULT

White central crown stripe • buffy-yellow eyebrow and face • grey cheek • grey nape with reddish streaks • brown streaked upperparts • buffy breast • narrow dark streaks on breast and sides • whitish belly • pointed tail feathers.

COMPARE TO

Sharp-tailed Sparrow, Henslow's Sparrow (see *Ammodramus* comparison pages 116–117).

LISTEN FOR

A hissing, insect-like song *tika-zzzzzzzzzz-tik*.

NATURE NOTES

Even when singing, this bird can be very difficult to see. In one research study, 86 singing males were found, but only eight of these were actually seen well enough to be visually identified.

SMALL

Adult

REAUME

Adult

RANGE
- ■ Breeding only
- Wintering only

Ammodramus nelsoni & Ammodramus caudacutus

Nelson's   SMALL

THESE TWO WERE ONCE considered to be the same species. The Nelson's
Sharp-tailed Sparrow breeds in the northern Midwest states and central
provinces, the Hudson Bay shoreline and Maine and the Maritime provinces
(see map). It is the one to watch for during migration in the Great Lakes
region. The Saltmarsh Sharp-tailed Sparrow breeds along the Atlantic coast
north to southern Maine, where it interbreeds with the Nelson's (just to make
things more confusing!). It is very rarely found inland from the coast.

ADULT NELSON'S

Bright buffy-orange face and eyebrow
• grey cheek and nape • grey central crown
stripe • brown streaked upperparts
• bright buffy orange breast and sides
• blurry brown streaks on breast and sides
• white belly • (the Atlantic population is
duskier overall).

ADULT SALTMARSH

Saltmarsh is very similar but has darker

and more defined breast streaks, less
defined streaks on the back and a more
distinctively white throat.

COMPARE TO

Le Conte's Sparrow (see *Ammodramus*
comparison pages 116–117).

LISTEN FOR

Song described by Rising (1996) as "the
sound of water dripped on a hot skillet, a
pschee-zipt." They often sing at night.

Saltmarsh

DANZENBAKER

Saltmarsh

DANZENBAKER

NATURE NOTES

The Nelson's Sharp-tailed Sparrow was first collected by an 18-year-old, Edward William Nelson, in 1874 and subsequently named for him. Unlike most sparrows, the Nelson's Sharp-tailed Sparrow does not form a pair bond during the breeding season and thus the female raises the young virtually single-handed (or should I say single-winged?).

Nelson's

SMALL

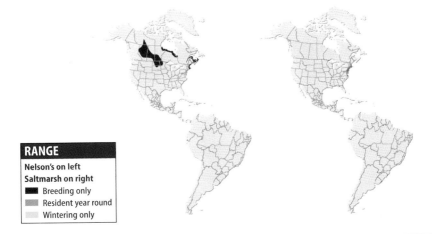

RANGE

Nelson's on left
Saltmarsh on right

■ Breeding only
■ Resident year round
□ Wintering only

Ammodramus maritimus

Adult WECHSLER

THE SEASIDE SPARROW, as its name suggests, is restricted to saltwater and brackish marshes of the Atlantic and Gulf of Mexico coasts. Wilson (in Studer, 1881) wrote, "When the high tides compel it to seek the shore, it courses along the margin, and among the holes and interstices of the weeds and sea-wrack, with a rapidity equaled only by the nimblest of our Sand-pipers." This foraging strategy seems to have an effect on this sparrow's edibility; it was noted by both Audubon and Nuttall that it was not good to eat because it tasted fishy.

ADULT

Grey head with indistinct brownish lateral crown stripes and eyeline • grey central crown stripe • *yellow lores* • *white or whitish throat* • dark malar stripe • *grey upperparts* • indistinct darkish streaks on back • brown wings and tail • *greyish-buff breast with blurry streaks* • buffy undertail coverts.

COMPARE TO

Nelson's and Saltmarsh Sharp-tailed Sparrows

LISTEN FOR

A quiet song that somewhat resembles a far-off Red-winged Blackbird.

NATURE NOTES

There are at least nine recognized subspecies of the Seaside Sparrow, two of which are extinct. One surviving

Singing adult

WECHSLER

Adult

DANZENBAKER

subspecies in southern Florida, the "Cape Sable Seaside Sparrow", will live in freshwater marshes as well as brackish water areas. The subspecies found along the north and central Atlantic coast, *A. maritimus maritimus*, is the one that is described above.

RANGE

- Breeding only
- Resident year round
- Wintering only

Passerella iliaca

Adult

A SINGLE FOX SPARROW stayed at my childhood bird feeders in Strathroy, Ontario, for a few consecutive winters. I loved to think that it was always the same one, and since many bird species do winter in the same spot each year, maybe it was. I enjoyed watching how its backwards kick-scratching sent leaves or snow flying as it looked for fallen seed under the feeder. Its rufous and grey feathers make this a very striking but remarkably well camouflaged sparrow. During spring migration, birders in the Great Lakes region may have a chance to hear the Fox Sparrow's beautiful song.

ADULT

A comparatively large sparrow • *grey head with rufous on crown and face* • *rufous streaked upperparts* • thin white wingbars • grey rump • white breast and belly • *rufous streaks on breast and sides* • *often a large breast spot.*

COMPARE TO

Song Sparrow, Vesper Sparrow, female Purple Finch, female House Finch, Hermit Thrush.

LISTEN FOR

Often described as the best singer of our sparrow species. The song is a rich series of whistles and short buzzy trills.

Adult MCCAW

Adult FLYNN

NATURE NOTES

The Fox Sparrow has many geographical variations, and ranges in color from the "Red Fox Sparrow" shown here to a very dark brown "Sooty Fox Sparrow" of coastal British Columbia. It is possible that this species will soon be split into three or four separate species, but Great Lakes region birders will have to be happy with the beautiful "Red Fox Sparrow" as it is the only one found in our area.

RANGE

- Breeding only
- Resident year round
- Wintering only

Melospiza melodia

Adult

"THERE IS A LARGE population right at my door; no time is wasted in going to and from the field of study and I am able to keep track of my subjects all the time…the song sparrow is an abundant, widely distributed, friendly and attractive bird." So wrote one of the best ornithologists of her time – Margaret Morse Nice – in 1937. She studied this common sparrow of backyard and garden, and you should, too. By knowing this common species well, you will be able to identify other, less commonly seen sparrows through comparison. It will also give you a chance to learn about its breeding biology and watch for different behaviors.

ADULT

Brown streaked upperparts • very thin white wingbars • white underparts • *thick brown streaks on breast and sides* • *usually a strong central breast spot* • *long, rounded tail* • pumps tail in flight.

COMPARE TO

Fox Sparrow, Vesper Sparrow, Savannah Sparrow, Lincoln's Sparrow, Purple Finch, House Finch, Rose-breasted Grosbeak, female Red-winged Blackbird.

LISTEN FOR

Song usually starts with three or four clear notes followed by a trill and then

Adult   MCCAW

some more jumbled notes, *Madge, Madge, Madge put on the tea kettle kettle kettle kettle*. Sometimes sings at night.

NATURE NOTES

Like the Fox Sparrow, there are many different subspecies of Song Sparrows, with the darkest ones being found on the west coast. Most Song Sparrows migrate south from the Great Lakes region in the winter, but a few stick around where they may visit feeders, and are often found in wet areas.

Adult   MCCAW

Juvenile   MCCAW

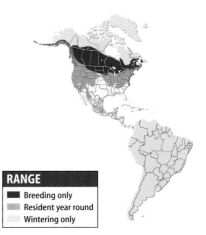

RANGE

■ Breeding only
■ Resident year round
  Wintering only

Melospiza lincolnii

Adult

FOR MOST GREAT LAKES region birders, the Lincoln's Sparrow is a species that is seen only during migration, though it does breed in a few southern Ontario localities. William Brewster (1936, in Bent 1968) describes it as "a keen, intelligent little traveler, evidently, quite alive to the fact that dangers threatened at all times, but too cool-headed and experienced to be subject to the needless and foolish panics which seize upon many of the smaller birds." Lincoln's Sparrows are remarkable for staying well hidden, but a careful observer, with patience, can often get quite a good look. These sparrows often raise their crown feathers when alert or concerned, giving their heads a bit of a peaked appearance.

ADULT

Thick grey eyebrow • *thin buffy eyering*
• brown streaked above • white throat
• *buffy breast and sides* • white belly
• *thin dark streaks on breast and sides*
• *often a small central breast spot.*

COMPARE TO

Song Sparrow, Vesper Sparrow, Swamp Sparrow.

LISTEN FOR

A bubbling song of jumbled trills that is similar to the House Wren's song.

Adult

FLYNN

NATURE NOTES

J.J. Audubon named this sparrow in 1834 for Thomas Lincoln, who saw the first specimen and, "with his usual unerring aim, he cut short its career." J. Murray and Doris Huetis Speirs (in Bent, 1968) know a great clue to finding this secretive sparrow." At Toronto, migrating White-crowned Sparrows and Lincoln's Sparrows usually arrive at the same time. As the former is more conspicuous and noticed first, keen bird students in the area immediately become alert to the possibility of Lincoln's lurking in the underbrush."

RANGE
- Breeding only
- Wintering only

Melospiza georgiana

Winter

"THE SWAMP SPARROW is not a public character. He will never be popular or notorious. He is too retiring to be much in the public eye, and too fond of the impassable bog and morass to have much human company; and so he comes and goes unheralded and to most people unknown." Well, to summarize Forbush (1929), this is a fairly shy sparrow. But it isn't too hard to find in the breeding season, especially with the addition of boardwalks in many parks that allow us to enter marshes and swamps easily. A patient observer in the right habitat has a good chance to hear, and maybe see, a Swamp Sparrow.

SUMMER ADULT

Reddish crown • *grey face and sides of neck* • white or whitish throat • brown streaked upperparts • *rufous wings* • grey breast • buffy sides • one study showed only 10 percent of breeding females had reddish crowns – most had brownish crowns instead • pumps tail in flight.

WINTER ADULT

Similar to summer except for • dark-streaked brown crown • faint streaks on breast • possible faint central breast spot • buffy wash on cheeks • (First winter more buffy wash on face.)

Summer

MCCAW

COMPARE TO

Lincoln's Sparrow, American Tree Sparrow, Chipping Sparrow, Field Sparrow, Song Sparrow.

LISTEN FOR

Song is a slow, musical trill, not as dry or fast as a Chipping Sparrow's song.

NATURE NOTES

Obviously, with the name "Swamp", this sparrow is comfortable near water. It will not only wade in shallow water, but will actually put its head under the surface to look for aquatic insects. Most Swamp Sparrows migrate south, but a few stay in the Great Lakes region in wet areas all winter.

Summer

MCCAW

RANGE

- Breeding only
- Resident year round
- Wintering only

White-striped morph
FLYNN

ALTHOUGH BEST KNOWN for its song, "home sweet Canada, Canada, Canada," the White-throated Sparrow is unique because it has a mating pattern like no other bird. There are two color morphs, white-striped and tan-striped, and males and females can be either morph. The unique part is the fact that a pair is usually made up of one of each color morph. This apparently occurs because white-striped males are aggressive compared to tan-striped males. Also, white-striped females sing, whereas tan-striped females do not. Because the white-striped females sing, the white-striped males are aggressive toward them and thus mate only with tan-striped females. This leaves the less aggressive tan-striped males to mate with the white-striped females.

ADULT WHITE-STRIPED MORPH

Black crown with white central stripe • *white eyebrow* • *yellow lores* • black eyeline • grey cheek • *white throat* • brown streaked back • brownish rump • white wingbars • grey breast • fairly large sparrow.

ADULT TAN-STRIPED MORPH

Similar to white-striped except for *dark brown stripes on head* • buffy *central crown stripe* • *tan eyebrow* • duller yellow lores • buffy wash on face and underparts • some have faint breast streaks.

50

Tan-striped morph   FLYNN

First winter   MCCAW

FIRST WINTER

Similar to adult tan-striped except for darker breast streaking • possible central breast spot.

SIMILAR SPECIES

White-crowned Sparrow, winter Swamp Sparrow.

LISTEN FOR

A clear whistled *home sweet Canada Canada Canada*.

NATURE NOTES

Obviously an opportunist, one White-throated Sparrow was seen to scavenge from the carcass of another of its own species. However, maybe it likes to eat too much, because Audubon wrote, "It is a plump bird, fattening almost to excess… and affords delicious eating, for which many are killed with blow guns." According to FLAP (Fatal Light Awareness Program), this species is the number one casualty of nighttime collisions with lit office buildings in Toronto (see page 106). In eight years, over 2600 were collected at the foot of office towers.

The White-throated Sparrow may be found in very small numbers in winter in the Great Lakes region.

RANGE	
■	Breeding only
▨	Resident year round
▢	Wintering only

Summer adult

RICHARDS

NOT TO BE OUTDONE by its cousin the White-throated Sparrow, the Harris's Sparrow also has a claim to fame. It is the only species of bird to breed only in Canada, mostly in the mainland parts of Nunavut, the Northwest Territories and northern Manitoba. It may be seen in the Great Lakes region during migration, but mostly in the western part of the area. It is a rare winter resident here as well.

SUMMER ADULT

Grey head • black crown, face, throat and upper breast • pink beak • thin white wing bars • brown streaked back • greyish brown rump • greyish breast • black streaks on sides • large for a sparrow.

WINTER ADULT

Similar to summer adult except for • buffy cheeks and eyebrow • less black on head.

FIRST WINTER

Similar to winter adult except for • white throat, often bordered by black.

COMPARE TO

House Sparrow, Lapland Longspur.

LISTEN FOR

Song is a series of two or three clear whistles on same pitch, similar in quality to White-throated Sparrow.

Winter adult

FLYNN

NATURE NOTES

No one knew what this sparrow's eggs looked like for a very long time and solving this mystery was one of North American ornithologists' great quests. Finally, in 1931, George M. Sutton found a nest with eggs near Churchill, Manitoba, almost one hundred years after the Harris's Sparrow was first discovered by Europeans.

First winter

SMALL

RANGE

- ■ Breeding only
- □ Wintering only

White-crowned Sparrow

Zonotrichia leucophrys

Adult

AT FIRST GLANCE, this sparrow is very similar to the white-striped morph of the White-throated Sparrow. But by taking a closer look, you will see that it has an all-pink beak and a gray throat and nape. The first winter plumage of this species looks quite different from the adult's, so reviewing its field marks before fall migration is a good idea for the beginner.

ADULT

Black crown • *white central crown stripe* • *white eyebrow* • *black eyeline* • *pink beak* • grey cheeks and neck • brownish streaked back • greyish brown rump • white wingbars • grey breast.

FIRST WINTER

Similar to Adult except for • *brown instead of black head stripes* • buffy eyebrow and central crown stripe • buffy cheeks.

COMPARE TO

White-throated Sparrow, Field Sparrow, American Tree Sparrow, Chipping Sparrow (see comparison pages, 114-115).

LISTEN FOR

A series of two or three clear whistles, with the first usually higher in pitch, followed by some buzzy notes. Described in Bezener (2000) as "*I gotta go wee-wee now.*"

First winter

MCCAW

White-crowned (left) and White-throated Sparrows (right) can often be found together during migration.

NATURE NOTES

Because of this species' abundance and conspicuous nature, it has been studied a great deal and has helped science learn a lot about physiology, breeding biology and geographic song variations. It is found across North America and is divided into five subspecies. In the Great Lakes region, it is a common migrant and a rare wintering bird.

MCCAW

RANGE
■ Breeding only
■ Resident year round
□ Wintering only

Junco hyemalis

Male

STEPHEN EATON NOTED that this sparrow was once described as "leaden skies above, snow below" (in Bent, 1968). A very appropriate description for likely the easiest sparrow in this book to identify. Once called the "Snowbird" or "Tomtit", the Dark-eyed Junco is a favorite visitor to winter bird feeders across the southern half of the Great Lakes region. It is always so exciting when the first juncos arrive at your feeder in autumn, especially when it is likely that at least some of the wintering individuals have been there before, as juncos often winter in the same area each year. There are many different subspecies of juncos across North America, but the common one in the Great Lakes region is the "Slate-colored Junco", *Junco hyemalis hyemalis* (see the following pages 58–59 for other subspecies).

NOTE

The following identification features can blend together, making some sexing and aging impossible.

ADULT

Pink beak • *dark grey upperparts, throat, breast and sides* • *white belly* and undertail coverts • *white outer tail feathers*.

Likely a female

MCCAW

♂ FIRST WINTER

Similar to adult male except for some brown on the head, back and wings.

♀ ADULT

Similar to adult male except paler overall with a *variable brownish wash* and lighter grey edges on wings.

♀ FIRST WINTER

Similar to first winter male but even more of a brownish wash on upperparts and especially on sides.

LISTEN FOR

A long trill on one pitch, similar to a Chipping Sparrow but more musical.

NATURE NOTES

There is one record of a junco hybridizing with a White-throated Sparrow (try and picture what the resultant young might have looked like!). Each of the Dark-eyed Junco wintering flocks has a well-established dominance hierarchy, and you can watch individuals assert their positions when they visit your feeder.

Very few individuals show thin wingbars.

MCCAW

RANGE
- ■ Breeding only
- ■ Resident year round
- □ Wintering only

Male "Oregon" Junco, *Junco hyemalis oreganus*, *montanus*, or *shufledti*. FAIRBAIRN

AT LEAST THREE other Dark-eyed Junco subspecies have been recorded in the Great Lakes region. Keep in mind that there is variation within our "Slate-colored" subspecies, especially with females. If you have juncos coming to your bird feeder, look closely at the flock and you will note variations between individuals.

"Grey-headed" Junco, *J.h. caniceps*. FLYNN

Female "Oregon" Junco, Occasional Rare Straggler, autumn to spring. FAIRBAIRN

"Pink-sided" Junco, *J.h. mearnsi.* FLYNN

Calcarius pictus

Winter

UNLIKE MANY SMALL birds that have a monogamous breeding strategy, the Smith's Longspur has a polygynandrous system. This means that most males mate with two or more females and most females mate with two or three males. Instead of spending their time holding territories, the males copulate with the females as many times as possible to ensure that their sperm, not a competitor's, fertilizes the eggs. In one week, a female may copulate over 350 times – more than any other bird species. Males help more than one female raise their young as well, since they may be the father of at least one of the nestlings in two or three nests. The Smith's Longspur can be found in the Great Lakes region (usually the western part) during migration.

♂ SUMMER ADULT

Black crown • long *white eyebrow* • *black cheek with a white patch in the middle* • *rich orange-buff side of neck and underparts* • upperparts brown with dark streaks • white patch on shoulder, white outer tail feathers • usually light legs.

♀ SUMMER ADULT

Similar to male, but without the black and white head pattern • brown crown with dark streaks • buffy eyebrow • dark border cheek • paler underparts.

Summer female   MCCAW

Summer male   SMALL

WINTER

Similar to summer female, but even duller
• some blurry streaking on breast
• whitish wingbars • thin rufous edging
on wing feathers • buffy belly.

COMPARE TO

First winter Smith's and first winter
Lapland Longspurs look very similar to
one another. Smith's Longspurs tend to
have lighter legs and are buffier overall,
especially on the belly. Lapland
Longspurs have a white belly, a dark-
bordered cheek and much more rufous
edging in the wing feathers. As well, the
Lapland Longspur tends to show less
white in its outer tail feathers.

LISTEN FOR

A series of weak thin whistles that
become stronger near the end. Song
described as having the same quality as a
Yellow Warbler.

NATURE NOTES

Male Smith's Longspurs are ready for
their active mating strategy – their testes
are twice as big as those of other male
longspur species.

RANGE

■ Breeding only
  Wintering only

Calcarius lapponicus

Winter

THE LAPLAND LONGSPUR is a migrant and winter visitor to the Great Lakes region. It is often found here in winter traveling in flocks with Snow Buntings or Horned Larks.

♂ SUMMER ADULT

Black cheeks, crown, throat and breast • white or yellowish eyeline • reddish nape bordered by white • yellow beak • black on sides • brownish streaked back • white outer tail feathers • white belly.

♀ SUMMER ADULT

Similar to summer adult male except for • little or no black on head, only a dusky breast band, dark border on cheek and darkish crown • *nape faint rufous •* streaks on sides • dusky pink beak • mid-wing feathers are edged rufous, giving a rufous patch effect.

♂ WINTER ADULT

Similar to summer adult female except for • buffier eyebrow and cheek • paler crown • First winter male and winter adult female similar but buffier overall.

♀ WINTER ADULT

Very buffy overall with a buffy breast band • little or no rufous on nape.

COMPARE TO

Winter Smith's Longspur (see "Compare To" on page 61).

LISTEN FOR

Song is a variable and jingling warble.

Summer female

RICHARDS

Summer male

SMALL

Winter

SMALL

RANGE

- Breeding only
- Wintering only

Plectrophenax nivalis

Winter

THE SNOW BUNTING breeds farther north than any other songbird in the world, all the way to the northernmost coasts of Canada and Greenland. To help keep the eggs warm, the male feeds the female while she incubates so she doesn't need to leave the nest very often. This decreases the chance of the embryos dying of the cold. It is in the winter season that most of us get to watch these delightful inhabitants of open areas. Thoreau (1853) welcomed their arrival: "These are the true winter birds for you, these winged snowballs. I could hardly see them, the air was so full of driving snow. What hardy creatures!"

♂ SUMMER ADULT	♀ SUMMER ADULT
All white head • black back • black-and-white wings • white underparts and outer tail feathers.	*Greyish mottled head • white throat • brownish grey mottled back • brownish grey and white wings • white underparts and outer tail feathers.*

Winter male FLYNN

Winter, showing white in wings and tail. FLYNN

♂ WINTER ADULT

Similar to summer adult female except for • greyish parts replaced by a brown wash • more white in wings • first winter male has less white in wings than adult male.

♀ WINTER

Similar to first winter males but with less white in wings.

LISTEN FOR

A repetitive warble of jumbled, raspy notes, fairly similar to Lapland Longspur.

Summer female SMALL

Summer male RICHARDS

RANGE

- ■ Breeding only
- ■ Resident year round
- ■ Wintering only

Cardinalis cardinalis

Male

A DEFINITE FAVORITE, the cardinal is a delightful bird to have around. Though the male offers a brilliant show of red plumage, the female is equally striking with her red-tipped, warm-colored garb. At the University of Guelph's Arboretum in Ontario, one of the most frequent bird questions I am asked is "How can I attract a cardinal to my yard?" Lots of native shrubs for cover and nesting sites plus a feeder full of sunflower seeds should do the trick. But don't complain to me when the singing male outside your bedroom window wakes you up at four in the morning!

♂ ADULT

All red with greyish red back • large crest • black face • red or orange beak • long, rounded tail.

♀ ADULT

Warm brown body • reddish crest, wings and tail • blackish face • orange beak • long, rounded tail.

LISTEN FOR

A series of rich, slurred whistles in a pattern such as ***Nice bright red birdy-birdy-birdy-birdy-birdy***. Songs can be quite variable across its range.

NATURE NOTES

One wild female was known to be at least 15 years and 9 months old, quite elderly for a small songbird. Historically, the

Female

MCCAW

cardinal was not a bird of the northern part of the Great Lakes region. Ontario's first record was in Chatham in 1849 and they have been increasing ever since.

Though I'm not trying to ruin its goody-two-shoes image, you should know that there is a record of a cardinal eating a field mouse!

Juvenile cardinals have dark beaks that gradually change to orange.

MCCAW

RANGE

Resident year round

Pheucticus ludovicianus

Summer adult male

MCCAW

A SUMMER VISITOR worth waiting for, this bird is described by Tyler (in Bent, 1968): "It sings a long phrase with a well-defined form like a pretty little poem, sung in the softest of tones full of delicacy and charm, a voice of syrupy sweetness like no other bird. It is the Rose-breasted Grosbeak, pleasing to both eye and ear." Though the male is bright, its preference for leafy trees can make it visually inaccessible at times.

♂ ADULT

Black head • *pink beak* • black back • *white rump* • *white wing patches* • *red triangle on breast* • *white underparts* • First summer males have brownish flight feathers and may have less black overall than adult males.

♀ ADULT

Brown crown • light central crown stripe • *white eyebrow* • brownish streaked upperparts • white wingbars • white underparts • *streaked breast and sides* • Winter females may have a buffy wash on breast. • First winter males similar to females but may have a rich orangy-buff breast.

Adult female   SMALL

COMPARE TO

Female Purple Finch, female Red-winged Blackbird.

LISTEN FOR

A series of rich whistles *cheer-up, cheery, cheerio, cheeru, cheerily...* like a fast American Robin who has had music lessons.

NATURE NOTES

When Thoreau (1910) saw his first Rose-breasted Grosbeak in 1853, he was very impressed: "How much it enhances the wildness and the richness of the forest to see in it some beautiful bird which you never detected before!"

First winter male   SMALL

RANGE	
■	Breeding only
	Wintering only

Passerina caerulea

Male   FLYNN

MOST OF THE Blue Grosbeak's breeding range is south of the Great Lakes region, but during spring migration, some individuals "overshoot" into many parts of our area. This species is very similar to the Indigo Bunting, so you must be very careful when trying to identify them (see comparison pages 118–119).

♂ ADULT

Dark blue overall • large heavy beak • black feathers around the base of the beak • *chestnut shoulder patch and wing bar.*

♀ ADULT

Brown overall • faint blue highlights in wings and tail • *light chestnut shoulder patch* (can be hard to see) and wingbar.

♂ FIRST SUMMER

Similar to adult female, but with variable blue patches all over.

♂♀ FIRST WINTER

Similar to adult female, but a richer brown overall.

COMPARE TO

Indigo Bunting (see comparison pages 118–119).

LISTEN FOR

A warble of rising and falling musical notes.

Female

SMALL

NATURE NOTES

Blue Grosbeaks favor quite large insects such as grasshoppers, crickets and even praying mantids and cicadas. The genus name for the Blue Grosbeak once was *Guiraca*, however, recent molecular analyses have revealed that it is actually a *Passerina* bunting, as is the Indigo Bunting.

First summer male

SMALL

RANGE

Breeding only

Wintering only

Passerina cyanea

Summer adult male

HERE IS A SINGER that doesn't restrict himself to just the morning. The male sings even in the heat of the afternoon, when most birds are taking a breather. One researcher calculated that a male Indigo Bunting sang an average of 4320 songs a day – for 61 days. That's 263,520 songs! No wonder the females end up doing almost all of the parental care.

♂ SUMMER ADULT

All brilliant blue, head a bit deeper in color.

♀ SUMMER

Brown overall • *faint blue highlights in wings and tail* • light colored throat • *faint, blurry streaks on breast* • whitish belly and undertail coverts.

♂ WINTER & FIRST SPRING

Similar to summer female except for varying amounts of blue patches throughout.

♀ WINTER

Similar to summer female except for being a bit warmer brown with fainter breast streaks.

COMPARE TO

Female Brown-headed Cowbird, Blue Grosbeak (see comparison pages 118–119).

LISTEN FOR

High, whistled, repeated phrases, much like, *fire-fire where-where there-there*.

Summer female

SMALL

NATURE NOTES

In low light, a male Indigo Bunting doesn't look very indigo; it looks brownish or black. This is because birds don't produce blue pigment in their feathers. While other feather colors such as red, yellow, orange and brown are pigments, blue is actually a structural color. This means that the blue we see is caused by the structure of the cells on the surface of the feather reflecting only blue light. So, a male indigo bunting needs enough light to be able to produce blue – and what a blue it is!

First spring male

SMALL

RANGE
■ Breeding only
  Wintering only

Spiza americana

Adult male

SMALL

THIS BIRD HAS a bit of an identity crisis – or rather, humans have a crisis in giving this bird an identity. It is currently listed in the Cardinal family, but some think it may fit better in the Blackbird family. The Great Lakes region is at the very northern edge of the Dickcissel's range, so they are not commonly seen here in all areas. In some years there is a small influx of them.

♂ ADULT

Grey head • yellowish eyebrow • some yellow below cheek • white throat • streaked back • *rufous shoulder patch • black V on yellow breast* • greyish sides • white belly and undertail coverts.

♀ ADULT

Similar to adult male except for • brownish wash where grey is • no black V on breast • less rufous on wing.

♀ FIRST WINTER

Similar to adult female except for • more brown overall • no rufous in wing • no or only slight yellow • fine streaks on breast.

COMPARE TO

Meadowlark, female House Sparrow.

LISTEN FOR

An insect-like, *dick dick dick ciss cissel*.

NATURE NOTES

A rare visitor to bird feeders in winter, usually found with House Sparrows.

Adult female

FLYNN

Adult male

SMALL

First winter female

SMALL

Female House Sparrow for comparison

MCCAW

RANGE
- Breeding only
- Wintering only

Pinicola enucleator

Male

THE STRIKING MALE Pine Grosbeak is a sight to behold against newly fallen snow. Thoreau (1851) called them "magnificent winter birds…with red or crimson reflections more beautiful than a steady bright red would be." This finch can be quite tame and allow close approach, giving you a good view. It is an irruptive migrant in the Great Lakes region, meaning that it irregularly comes to the area when its food supply of conifer seeds is low in the north.

♂ ADULT

Bright raspberry-red head, breast sides, and rump • short black eyeline • streaked back • *white wingbars* • grey belly and undertail coverts.

♀ ADULT

Similar to adult male except for • grey overall, no red • olive head and rump • grey throat • First winter female duller overall.

♂ FIRST YEAR MALE

Similar to "typical" female except for rusty coloring replacing the olive.

♀ "RUSSET"

Similar to "typical" female except for rusty coloring replacing the olive.

LISTEN FOR

A musical series of soft whistles.

COMPARE TO

White-winged Crossbill.

Female

MCCAW

NATURE NOTES

The Pine Grosbeak sometimes incorporates other birds' sounds in its own songs. These have included the calls of the Hairy Woodpecker, Gray Jay, American Robin and redpoll. When some Pine Grosbeaks were moved to an aviary outside of their normal range for research purposes, they incorporated the newly heard songs of Northern Cardinals and Carolina Wrens.

First year male or "russet" female

REAUME

RANGE
Resident year round
Wintering only

Carpodacus purpureus

Male

THOREAU (1842) WRITES of the Purple Finch, "It has the crimson hues of the October evenings, and its plumage still shines as if it had caught and preserved some of their tints (beams?). Many a serene evening lies snugly packed under its wing." This brilliant finch has been described as being dipped in raspberry juice. It breeds throughout much of the Great Lakes region. In winter, it is a regular visitor to feeders.

♂ ADULT

Raspberry-red head, breast, sides and rump • reddish wash on back and wings • brownish cheek • brown streaks on back • faint to distinct brown streaks on flanks • *white belly and undertail coverts* • reddish wingbars.

♀ ADULT   ♂ FIRST YEAR

Brown head • *white eyebrow and throat* • brown upperparts • streaked back • *white underparts* • *dark streaks on throat, breast and sides* • thin white wingbars.

COMPARE TO

House Finch (see comparison pages 120–121), female Rose-breasted Grosbeak, Song Sparrow, Savannah Sparrow.

Female or first year male

MCCAW

LISTEN FOR

A musical warble of varied, rich notes.

NATURE NOTES

Purple Finches have a fondness for the buds and nectar of blooming trees in the spring. Males have three types of songs – a warbling song, a territorial song and a "vireo" song. The last is named for its resemblance to the song of the Red-eyed Vireo.

A male with distinct streaks on flanks.

FLYNN

RANGE
■ Breeding only
■ Resident year round
□ Wintering only

Carpodacus mexicanus

Adult male

THE YEAR 1940 was an important one for the House Finch. In that year, a bunch of illegally kept "Hollywood Finches" was released on Long Island, New York. Their new home was to their liking, and in 1972 the first one in Ontario showed up at Prince Edward Point. It is now a common finch in the Great Lakes region and at some point will likely spread across the continent to its original western range. It is a suburbanite that loves to nest in the Colorado Blue Spruce in your front yard, in hanging flower pots on your porch or even in the wreath on your front door.

♂ ADULT

Red forehead, eyebrow, breast and rump • otherwise brown overall • streaks on back • *whitish belly, sides and undertail coverts* • *brown streaks on lower breast and sides* • whitish wingbars • short, rounded beak • some individuals have orange or yellow that replaces the red.

♀ ADULT   ♂ FIRST YEAR

Brown head and upperparts • streaked back • dirty white underparts • brown streaks on breast and sides • whitish wingbars • short, rounded beak.

COMPARE TO

Purple Finch (see comparison pages 120–121), Song Sparrow and Savannah Sparrow.

Female

FLYNN

LISTEN FOR

A musical but raspy warble.

NATURE NOTES

This species is susceptible to a disease that causes its eyes to become swollen or crusty. It is called mycoplasmal conjunctivitis and, though found in poultry, it is new for songbirds. American Goldfinches and Purple Finches have also been seen with this disease. Because it may be transmitted at bird feeders, it is a good idea to clean them periodically, especially if you see a diseased bird visiting them.

SMALL

Yellow variant male showing signs of eye disease.

RANGE

Resident year round

Loxia curvirostra

Adult male   MCCAW

CROSSBILLS ARE THE parrots of the songbird world. Thoreau (1860) wrote that Red Crossbills "were very parrot-like both in color (especially the male, greenish and orange, etc.) and in their manner of feeding – holding the hemlock cones in one claw and rapidly extracting the seeds with their bills, thus trying one cone after another very fast." They use their crossed beaks to spread apart the scales of unopened conifer cones so that they can get their tongue in to pull out a seed.

♂ ADULT

Dull red body • dark wings and tail • whitish undertail coverts • *crossed beak*.

♂ FIRST YEAR

Similar to adult male except for dull orange replacing the red.

♀ ADULT

Similar to adult male except olive-yellow to olive-grey replacing the red.

COMPARE TO

White-winged Crossbill, Purple Finch.

LISTEN FOR

A series of warbles and trills.

Female

FAIRBAIRN

NATURE NOTES

There are eight types of Red Crossbills in North America and each type has its own distinctive call and food preference. As well, each type has a slightly different beak and body size, which likely depends on what its preferred conifer cone is. So, it is possible that they could someday be separate species; this would be a real challenge to birders (and to those of us who write bird books!).

First year male

SMALL

RANGE
Resident year round

Loxia leucoptera

Adult male

BECAUSE CROSSBILLS ARE so tied to conifer cones for food, they have to be ready to move around to find tree populations with a heavy cone crop. Crossbills have likely "helped" trees evolve to stagger their cone crops – if the trees produced the same amount each year, crossbill numbers would likely stabilize to eat almost all of the seeds. By having bumper crops every few years, trees have a better chance of swamping their seed predators with so much food that they can't eat it all. Thus, species like the White-winged Crossbill have to move around to find food and so are only found in the Great Lakes region when their northern food sources are low.

♂ ADULT

Pink body (redder in summer) • black wings and tail • *bold white wingbars* • greyish sides • whitish undertail coverts • *crossed beak.*

♂ FIRST YEAR

Same as adult male except for brownish wings and orange replacing pink.

♀ ADULT

Brownish-grey streaked body • variable olive-yellow wash on breast and rump • blurry streaks on breast • brownish wings and tail • bold white wingbars • whitish undertail coverts.

Female

FAIRBAIRN

COMPARE TO

Red Crossbill, Pine Grosbeak, Pine Siskin.

LISTEN FOR

A series of warbles and trills, somewhat harsher than Red Crossbill.

NATURE NOTES

Crossbills could be considered to be righties or lefties. If their lower mandible curves to the left side of the upper mandible, they usually hold their cone with the right foot. If the lower mandible curves to the right, they use their left foot. This likely makes their foraging technique as efficient as possible.

RANGE

Resident year round

Carduelis flammea

Adult male

EVERYONE WITH A BIRD feeder who has had these finches visit waits each year for them to return. The pink of the males seems to glow. Thoreau (1855) wrote, "What a rich contrast! Tropical colors, crimson breasts on cold white snow! Such etherealness, such delicacy in their forms, such ripeness in their colors, in this stern and barren season!" And even though they look delicate, they can survive pretty severe winter conditions. To do this they may have to eat more than 40 percent of their body weight in seeds per day.

♂ ADULT

(Southern subspecies, *C. f. flammea*)
• *black face and chin* • *red forecrown*
• streaked back • *white wingbars* • usually streaked rump • white underparts
• *variable bright pink wash on breast and rump* • dark streaks on sides • thin streaks on undertail coverts.

♀ ADULT

Similar to adult male except for • no pink (or very little) • more heavily streaked • smaller red forecrown • first year female may have a slight brown wash to upperparts and sides. • (Common Redpolls of the Greenland or Greater subspecies, *C. f. rostrata*, are larger, browner and darker overall. When seen in the Great Lakes region, they are usually in a flock of wintering Southern Common Redpolls.)

Female   REAUME

Male   MCCAW

Male   MCCAW

COMPARE TO

Hoary Redpoll (see comparison pages 122–123), Pine Siskin.

LISTEN FOR

A series of varied, twittering trills.

NATURE NOTES

The name "redpoll" refers to the red patch on the crown, or "poll," of these birds. Wintering Common Redpoll flocks may have Hoary Redpolls in their midst.

RANGE

■ Breeding only
■ Resident year round
□ Wintering only

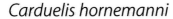

Carduelis hornemanni

Adult

REAUME

TWO SUBSPECIES OF Hoary Redpoll can be found in the Great Lakes region in winter. The "Southern Hoary Redpoll," *C. h. exilipes*, is more commonly seen than the "Greenland" or "Hornemann's" Hoary Redpoll, *C. h. hornemanni*. Some researchers believe that there are four species of redpoll (Common, Greater, Hoary and Hornemann's), while others group them all into one species. Variations between individuals of each group make identification tricky and sometimes not possible.

♂ ADULT

("Southern Hoary Redpoll," *C. h. exilipes*)
• *black face and chin* • red forecrown
• *stubby, short beak "pushed in face"*
• streaked back • *whitish border where wing meets the back* • white wingbars
• *usually unstreaked, white rump*
• white underparts • may have light pink on breast and on rump • thin, faint streaks on sides • *no (or only a few) thin streaks on undertail coverts.*

♀ ADULT

Similar to adult males except for • no pink
• heavier streaking • first year female may have a slight brownish ash to upperparts and sides • ("Hornemann's Hoary Redpoll" is larger and whiter).

COMPARE TO

Common Redpoll, Pine Siskin (see comparison pages 122-123).

Hoary Redpoll

A Hoary Redpoll (left) with a Common Redpoll (see comparison pages 122–123).

REAUME

LISTEN FOR

A series of varied, twittering trills.

Adult

SMALL

RANGE

◼ Breeding only
  Wintering only

89

Adult

MCCAW

THIS SMALL FINCH can be very tame, especially if it gets used to a bird feeder. In some cases, they may even land on you. The siskins coming to E.R. Davis's (1926) feeder became even bolder than that. "In a short time the siskins discovered this opening in a window pane, and one after another would come right into my kitchen. Now and then some members would elect to spend the night in the warm room, sleeping on the clothes-line." Talk about making yourself at home!

♂ ADULT

Thin, pointy beak • brownish streaked upperparts • *yellowish to white wingbar* • *bright yellow wingstripe seen in flight* on both sides of wing • white underparts • dark streaks on breast, sides and undertail coverts • yellow in tail.

♀ ADULT

Similar to male except for • less yellow in wing and tail • white wingbar.

COMPARE TO

Common Redpoll, female Purple and House Finches.

LISTEN FOR

A long, chattering series of rising raspy trills.

NATURE NOTES

Pine Siskins can be quite quarrelsome at the feeder and often lunge at each other.

Adult

MCCAW

Adult

FLYNN

RANGE

■ Breeding only
■ Resident year round
□ Wintering only

Carduelis tristis

Summer male

IT IS TRULY A JOY to have American Goldfinches with us throughout the year in the Great Lakes region. Interestingly, though, the birds that we have in the summer migrate south, and the ones we have in the winter are from farther north. They often nest in suburban areas (as well as forest edges and scrubby habitats), so we can watch their entire life cycle right in the backyard.

♂ SUMMER

Bright yellow head and body • *black forehead* • orange beak • *black wings and tail* • white wingbar • white rump and undertail coverts • extensive white spots in tail.

♀ SUMMER

Olive green upperparts • yellowish-olive underparts • pink bill • dark brownish black wings and tail • *white or buffy wingbar* • white undertail coverts • extensive white spots in tail.

♂ WINTER

Similar to Summer Adult Female except for • greyer overall • dusky beak • less yellow on breast • a yellow shoulder patch (may be concealed) • black wings and tail • may have some black spots on forehead.

♂ FIRST WINTER

Similar to winter adult male except for • no yellow shoulder • duller or browner overall • dark brownish-black wings and tail • buffier wingbars.

Summer female

SMALL

Winter

FLYNN

♀ WINTER

Similar to winter adult male except for •
no yellow shoulder • duller or browner
overall • dark brownish-black wings and
tail • buffer wingbars.

LISTEN FOR

A long, warbling series of twitters and
trills.

COMPARE TO

Evening Grosbeak and Pine Siskin.

NATURE NOTES

American Goldfinches nest late in the
season compared to most other
songbirds in the Great Lakes region. This
is likely an adaptation to food supply,
especially as one of the goldfinch's
favorite foods is thistle seeds, which are
most abundant in July and August, when
they breed. Another advantage to nesting
late is the fact that by late June most
female Brown-headed Cowbirds have
stopped laying their eggs in other birds'
nests, so few goldfinch nests are
parasitized.

Molting male in spring.

MCCAW

RANGE

- Breeding only
- Resident year round
- Wintering only

Coccothraustes vespertinus

Male

LIKE THE AMERICAN Goldfinch, the male Evening Grosbeak uses yellow to make his plumage bold and beautiful. But, unlike the goldfinch, he keeps it all year long. The female, too, is a striking bird, with muted splashes of color. This grosbeak's feeding habits are legendary, as Brunton (in McNichol & Cranmer-Byng, 1994) notes: "The Evening Grosbeak's seemingly inexhaustible appetite for sunflower seeds at winter feeders caused the late John Bird to coin a graphic nickname for them in the mid-1960s: he called them 'Greedies.'"

♂ ADULT

Dark brown head blending to yellow lower back and belly • Yellow eyebrow and forehead • pale beak • large white wing patch on black wings • black tail.

♀ ADULT

Greyish head and body • dusky lores • yellowish wash on sides and nape • grey and white patches on black wings • black tail with white tail spots • white undertail coverts.

LISTEN FOR

A series of musical whistled notes.

Female

MCCAW

COMPARE TO

American Goldfinch is much smaller.

NATURE NOTES

This species wasn't common in the eastern part of North America until the late-1800s; it was first found in Toronto in 1854. One idea as to why they may have moved east relates to logging. As logged areas started to regenerate, two pioneer species, the pin cherry and choke cherry, became more common, and they are a favorite food of the Evening Grosbeak. Some attribute the extension of its range to planting of the Manitoba Maple, whose seeds are another one of the Evening Grosbeak's favorites. Taverner (1921) called this planting a "baited highway" because it encouraged this species to follow the trees. Because

Evening Grosbeaks like maple buds, maple keys and even maple sap, one of their first names was "Sugar-bird."

RANGE

Resident year round
Wintering only

Passer domesticus

Summer male

WELL, HERE WE HAVE probably the most disliked bird in North America. But we must always keep in mind that we brought it here. One hundred House Sparrows were released in Brooklyn, New York, in 1851. They were also introduced later in other cities, including Ottawa and Halifax, as an insect control agent. They are now found across the continent and have quite an impressive worldwide distribution. If you think about most of the successfully introduced birds, such as House Sparrows, European Starlings and Rock Doves, you will notice that they are filling niches that were largely vacant. While they can be destructive to native species, we are more so. And both humans and House Sparrows are here to stay. We might as well start thinking of both of us as part of North America's fauna and do what we can to help nature keep the balance.

Female   MCCAW

Winter male   FLYNN

♂ SUMMER

Grey crown • *black face, chin and breast*
• black bill • rich brown upperparts
• streaked back • white wingbar
• greyish white cheek, sides, belly and
undertail coverts.

♂ WINTER

Similar to Summer Male except for
• duller overall • much less black on face
and breast • pale yellow beak.

♀ ADULT

Greyish-brown head and body • buffy
eyebrow • pale beak • streaked back • thin
wingbars.

COMPARE TO

Harris's Sparrow, winter Chipping Sparrow.

LISTEN FOR

A series of chirps.

NATURE NOTES

House Sparrows can adapt well to many
situations that result in food. During an
outbreak of June and/or Japanese Beetle
grubs in my lawn, the local sparrows
learned that the resident male American

Robin was adept at finding and digging
out the grubs. The robin would fling soil
about until he threw the grub out, at
which time the sparrows would rush in
and steal it. The robin soon learned that
sparrows on the ground nearby would
steal his grubs, so he would stop digging
when they were around. Subsequently,
the sparrows learned that if they just flew
back and forth over the lawn, the robin
would keep on digging and they could
still rush in and try to grab the grub
before the robin got it.

RANGE
Resident year round

Vagrants & stragglers

OVER 80 SPECIES of towhees, sparrows, cardinals, buntings and finches have been recorded in Canada and the U.S. In the Great Lakes region, the following species are not common occurrences. The status given to each of them is from *Ross James' Annotated Checklist of the Birds of Ontario,* 2nd Edition – a great resource book on the occurrence of birds in this region.

> **KEY**
>
> **Occasional** – expected most years, but not every year
> **Rare** – difficult to find
> **Straggler** – irregularly wandering into Ontario
> **Vagrant** – five or fewer records exist for Ontario

Green-tailed Towhee

Pipilo chlorurus **Vagrant**

FLYNN

This species is smaller than the other towhees in this book. It breeds in the western states and is a vagrant in the Great Lakes region. Note its rufous crown and green wings and tail.

Occasional, rare straggler | *Pipilo maculatus*

Along with the Eastern Towhee, the Spotted Towhee used to be a subspecies of what was once called the Rufous-sided Towhee. This western bird is an occasional straggler in the Great Lakes region, so be sure to check all towhees for spots!

FAIRBAIRN

Cassin's Sparrow

Vagrant | *Aimophila cassinii*

This secretive sparrow breeds in the south-central states. It is a vagrant in the Great Lakes region, with records during both spring and fall migration. It has been recorded in Illinois, Indiana, Michigan and Ontario.

SMALL

Bachman's Sparrow

Occasional, rare straggler | *Aimophila aestivalis*

A bird of the open pine forest of the southeastern states, the Bachman's Sparrow was an occasional, rare straggler in the Great Lakes region. Its normal range has been shrinking and thus it is even less likely to be here now.

SMALL

Spizella breweri

This close relative of the Chipping Sparrow and Clay-colored Sparrow breeds in the western states, southern Alberta and even parts of Yukon Territory. It has been recorded in Minnesota, Illinois and Michigan.

SMALL

Black-throated Sparrow

Amphispiza bilineata   *Vagrant*

The Black-throated Sparrow is a desert species that is usually found in the western states. It has been recorded in Minnesota, Wisconsin, Illinois, Michigan, Ohio and Ontario.

SMALL

Lark Bunting

Calamospiza melanocorys   *Occasional, rare straggler*

The Lark Bunting is an occasional, rare straggler in the Great Lakes region and has been recorded in all seasons. It breeds in the southern parts of the central provinces and in many central states. It has been recorded in all the states that touch the Great Lakes. The one shown here is an adult male.

MCCAW

100

Vagrant

Ammodramus bairdii

This relative of the Grasshopper Sparrow has been listed as a vagrant in most of the Great Lakes region. Though it is more common in the western part of our region, it has been recorded as far east as New York state. It breeds in the southern parts of the central provinces and in the north-central states.

MCCAW

Golden-crowned Sparrow

Occasional, rare straggler

Zonotrichia atricapilla

This relative of the White-throated and White-crowned Sparrows is considered an occasional, rare straggler. The one shown here is in its winter plumage.

SMALL

McCown's Longspur

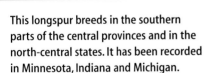

Calcarius mccownii

This longspur breeds in the southern parts of the central provinces and in the north-central states. It has been recorded in Minnesota, Indiana and Michigan.

SMALL

Calcarius ornatus **Vagrant**

This vagrant to the Great Lakes region breeds in the southern parts of the central provinces and in the north-central states. It has been recorded in many of the Great Lake states and Ontario.

SMALL

Black-headed Grosbeak

Pheucticus melanocephalus **Occasional, rare straggler**

This species sometimes hybridizes with the Rose-breasted Grosbeak where their ranges meet in the Great Plains. Females can be especially difficult to distinguish from Rose-breasted Grosbeaks. The Black-headed Grosbeak is an occasional, rare straggler in the Great Lakes region. An adult male is shown here.

SMALL

Lazuli Bunting

Passerina amoena **Vagrant**

The Lazuli Bunting is closely related to the Indigo Bunting and hybrids have been know to occur. It breeds in the southern parts of the western provinces and all the western states. It has been recorded as far east as New York state. A female is pictured here to show how similar it is to a female Indigo Bunting.

SMALL

102

Vagrant   *Passerina versicolor*

This species was added to the Great Lakes region list when a female or immature male visited Long Point, Ontario, in May 1995. This bird was a long way from home – they breed in the very south of the south-central states and throughout Mexico! An adult male is pictured here.

FLYNN

Painted Bunting

Vagrant   *Passerina ciris*

The Painted Bunting has been recorded in all the Great Lakes states and Ontario. It breeds in the southern states. The adult male, shown here, is a striking bird that would be hard to misidentify. The adult female is greenish overall but with a yellow wash below.

SMALL

Brambling

Vagrant   *Fringilla montifringilla*

This Eurasian finch is a vagrant in the Great Lakes region. This species has shown up at bird feeders in many places across North America in winter. These individuals are thought to be fall migrants that have crossed the Bering Sea to Alaska and then come south.

FLYNN

Leucosticte tephrocotis **Occasional, rare straggler**

This is an occasional, rare straggler from western North America. Both the Hepburn's subspecies (*L.t. littoralis*), which has a gray cheek, and the Gray-crowned or Interior subspecies (*L.t. tephrocotis*) have been recorded in the Great Lakes region. The Gray-crowned is shown here.

SMALL

Cassin's Finch

Carpodacus cassinii **Vagrant**

This vagrant species from the west is remarkably like a Purple Finch. The male Cassin's Finch (shown here) has more of a "red-capped" look than the Purple. Females are more difficult, with Cassin's Finches tending to have less of an eyebrow, finer streaks on the breast and more streaks on the undertail coverts.

SMALL

Vagrant

Carduelis psaltria

There is only one record of a Lesser Goldfinch in the Great Lakes region, and that was a female in Toronto, Ontario, in August 1982. This species breeds in the southwestern states. A female is shown here.

SMALL

Eurasian Tree Sparrow

Vagrant

Passer montanus

The Eurasian Tree Sparrow is an introduced resident of the St. Louis area of Missouri and Illinois. Both the male and the female of this species resemble the male House Sparrow with the addition of a black cheek patch and a brown crown.

DANZENBAKER

What can I do to help sparrows & finches?

MCCAW

Song Sparrow nest

MANY SPARROWS AND FINCHES ARE easily attracted to feeders throughout the year. A combination of white millet, black oil sunflower seeds and nyger seed seems to be the best mixture to attract the largest number of species. This way you can watch them interact with each other and with other species of birds, including their predators.

Naturalizing your backyard or your workplace's outdoor space also helps both breeding and migrating birds because certain native plants provide cover and nesting sites as well as food. There are many places to see examples and take courses about naturalization, such as the Gosling Wildlife Gardens at the University of Guelph (Ontario) Arboretum (519-824-4120 ext. 52113, www.uoguelph.ca/~arboretum). There are also many books on attracting wildlife to your site.

You can also give support to national, state and provincial parks and conservation areas, as well as naturalist groups. The organization FLAP (Fatal Light Awareness Program) works to prevent nighttime migrants such as sparrows from flying into lit city buildings (416-366-3527, www.flap.org). Not only do FLAP members go around the streets of downtown Toronto before dawn to save injured migrating birds, they also have encouraged many big city businesses to turn off their lights at night to decrease the number of migrant fatalities each year.

MCCAW

References

MANY REFERENCES on sparrows and finches are available that can provide more information on their identification and natural history. *Sparrows of the United States and Canada,* by James D. Rising and David Beadle, is highly recommended. There are two different books, one with plates (paintings) of the birds and one with photographs. A new and almost complete series, *The Birds of North America,* edited by A. Poole and F. Gill, includes heaps of information that has been collected by the scientific community on birds and their natural history. *Finches and Sparrows,* by Peter Clement and *Sparrows and Buntings,* by C. Byers, J. Curson and U. Olsson, are also recommended for those wanting to delve into more detail.

All the Birds of North America by Round Table Press, Inc. 1997, Harper Perennial.

Annotated Checklist of the Birds of Ontario, second edition by R. D. James, 1991, Royal Ontario Museum.

Atlas of the Breeding Birds of Ontario by M.D. Cadman, P.F.J. Eagles and F.M. Helleiner, 1987, University of Waterloo Press.

The Audubon Society Encyclopedia of North American Birds by John K. Terres, 1991, Wings Books.

The Birder's Handbook by Ehrlich, Dobkin and Wheye, 1988, Fireside/Simon & Schuster Inc.

The Birds of Canada - revised edition by W. Earl Godfrey, 1986, National Museums of Canada

Birds of Massachusetts and New England States by E.H. Forbush, 1929.

The Birds of North America, The Academy of Natural Sciences of Philadelphia and The American Ornithologists' Union. (AOU)

Birds of Ontario by Andy Bezener. 2000, Lone Pine Publishing.

Check-list of North American Birds, 1998 by (AOU)

COSEWIC status reports Committee On the Status of Endangered Wildlife In Canada.

The Dictionary of American Bird Names, revised edition by E.A. Choate, 1985, Harvard Common Press.

A Field Guide To the Birds, R.T. Peterson, 1934, Houghton Mifflin Co.

Field Guide to the Birds of North America by the National Geographic Society, 1987.

Field Identification: Lincoln's Sparrow by Kenn Kaufman, Birder's World, February, 1998.

Field Identification: Savannah Sparrow by Kenn Kaufman, Birder's World, December, 1994.

Field Identification: Vesper Sparrow by Kenn Kaufman, Birder's World, February, 1999.

Finches and Sparrows by Peter Clement, 1993. Princeton Univ. Press.

A Guide to Field Identification: Birds of North America by Robbins, Bruun and Zim, 1966, Golden Press.

A Guide to the Identification and Natural History of The Sparrows of the United States and Canada by J.D. Rising, 1996. Academic Press Inc.

Identifying Common and Hoary Redpolls in Winter by Dave Czaplak. Birding Vol.27, Number 6, Dec. 1995.

Kaufman Focus Guides: Birds of North America by Kenn Kaufman. 2000. Houghton Mifflin Company

Life Histories of North American Cardinals, Grosbeaks, Buntings, Towhees, Finches, Sparrows, and Allies by A.C. Bent and Collaborators, 1968, parts 1, 2 & 3. U.S. National Museum.

Field Guide to North American Birds – Eastern Region, National Audubon Society by J. Bull and J. Farrand, Jr., 1994 Alfred A. Knoft, Inc.

Ontario Birds – various articles from the *Ontario Field Ornithologists* magazine.

Ornithology in Ontario, Ed. by McNicholl & Cranmer-Byng. 1994. HawkOwl Publishing.

Peterson Field Guides: Advance Birding by Kenn Kaufman, 1990, Houghton Mifflin Company.

Peterson Field Guides: Eastern Birds by R.T. Peterson, Houghton Mifflin Co.

Lives of North American Birds by Kenn Kaufman, *Peterson Natural History Companions:* 1996. Houghton Mifflin.

Pilgrim at Tinker Creek by Annie Dillard, 1974, Harper & Row.

Recognizable Forms: Subspecies of the Dark-eyed Junco by Ron Pittaway. Ontario Birds December 1993, Vol. 11, Number 3.

Seasonal Status of Birds: Point Pelee National Park and Vicinity compiled by J.R. Graham, 1996.

The Seed-eaters by Michael Runtz. Nature Canada, Winter 1999.

The Sibley Guide to Birds, National Audubon Society, by David A. Sibley. 2000. Alfred A. Knopf

Sparrows and Buntings: An Identification Guide to the Sparrows and Buntings of North America and the World by C. Byers, Jon Curson and Urban Olsson. 1995, Houghton Mifflin Co.

Sparrows of the United States and Canada: The Photographic Guide by David Beadle and James Rising, 2002. Academic Press.

Stokes Field Guide to Birds: Eastern Region by D. & L. Stokes, 1996. Little, Brown and Company.

Stokes Nature Guides: Bird Behavior Vol. I, II & III. by D. & L. Stokes, 1979, 1983 & 1989. Little, Brown and Company.

Studies in the Life History of the Song Sparrow Vol. I & II by Margaret Morse Nice. Dover Publications,. 1964.

Thoreau on Birds: Notes on New England Birds from the journals of Henry David Thoreau. 1910. Beacon Press.

Cheat sheets

THIS LIST IS TO BE USED as a guideline only; it does not cover all features needed to identify all sparrows and "sparrow-like" finches. It does, however, highlight many important field marks. Before you read this, consider making a chart, key or list like this on your own. By doing it yourself, you will learn and remember the field marks more easily – trust me!

UNSTREAKED (OR VERY FAINTLY STREAKED) BREAST

Rufous Crown
   Central breast spot

☐ **American Tree Sparrow** • bicolored beak

☐ **Lark Sparrow** • white central crown stripe, rufous cheek

No central breast spot

☐ **Chipping Sparrow** • black eyeline, white eyebrow, black beak

☐ **Swamp Sparrow** • reddish brown wings, no wingbars, brown rump

☐ **Field Sparrow** • pink beak, white eyering

☐ **White-crowned Sparrow (immature)** • pinkish beak, large size

No Rufous Crown
   Black and white (or tan) stripes on crown

☐ **White-throated Sparrow** • yellow lores, defined white throat

☐ **White-crowned Sparrow (adult)** • pink bill, gray face and nape

No black and white stripes on head
• Whitish central crown stripe

☐ **Clay-colored Sparrow** • gray breast, buffy cheek with dark outline

☐ **Grasshopper Sparrow** • buffy breast, whitish eyering

• No whitish central crown stripe

☐ **Dark-eyed Junco** • gray above, white below

☐ **Snow Bunting** • a lot of white throughout

☐ **House Sparrow** ♂ • black throat and lores

☐ **House Sparrow** ♀ • buffy eyebrow, brownish eyeline

☐ **Indigo Bunting** ♀ • plain brownish face

☐ **Dickcissel** ♀ **(first winter)** • malar stripe, faint thin breast streaks

☐ **American Goldfinch** ♀ • yellowish throat

DISTINCTLY STREAKED BREAST AND/OR SIDES

Distinct white or whitish background on breast
   Black throat

☐ **Harris' Sparrow** • pink beak, black crown, black in breast

☐ **Common Redpoll** • reddish forecrown, streaks on undertail coverts

☐ **Hoary Redpoll** • reddish forecrown, unstreaked undertail coverts

Cheat sheets

DISTINCTLY STREAKED BREAST AND/OR SIDES (continued)

No Black throat

☐ **Fox Sparrow** • very rufous, large size, boldly streaked with rufous

☐ **Vesper Sparrow** • chestnut shoulder, eyering

☐ **Rose-breasted Grosbeak** ♀ • large size, bold white eyebrow

☐ **Purple Finch** ♀ • bold white eyebrow, notched tail

☐ **House Finch** ♀ • plain face, dull brown

☐ **Pine Siskin** • often yellow in wing, thin beak (for a finch)

☐ **Savannah Sparrow** • short, notched tail, usually yellowish eyebrow

☐ **Song Sparrow** • long, rounded tail, usually a central breast spot

Buffy background on breast
Buffy color surrounding gray cheek

☐ **Le Conte's Sparrow** • streaked nape

☐ **Nelson's Sharp-tailed Sparrow** • clear gray nape

No Gray Cheek

☐ **Lincoln's Sparrow** • gray eyebrow

☐ **Henslow's Sparrow** • olive-green head and neck, reddish brown wings

☐ **Lapland Longspur (winter)** • brownish or whitish eyebrow, dark ear patch

☐ **House Finch** ♀ • plain face, dull brown

Index

Sparrows with Rufous Crowns Comparison

Sparrows with
Rufous Crowns
Comparison

Chipping Sparrow (summer) • page 20 — MCCAW

Swamp Sparrow (summer) • page 48 — MCCAW

American Tree Sparrow • page 18 — MCCAW

Field Sparrow • page 24 — FLYNN

White Crowned Sparrow (first winter) • page 54 — MCCAW

	Eyebrow	Eyeline	Eyering	Beak	Breast	Wing	Overall size
American Tree	Gray	Rufous – behind eye only	Very thin and broken	Bicolored	Plain with central spot	White wingbars	Medium
Chipping	White	Black	None	Black	Plain	White	Small
Field	Gray	Rufous – behind	Complete	Pink	Plain	White wingbars	Small
Swamp	Gray	Dark	None or very thin and broken	Dark with yellowish base	Very faint streaks on sides	Rufous, no wingbars	Medium
First winter White-crowned	Grayish buff	Rufous	None	Pink	Plain	White wingbars	Large

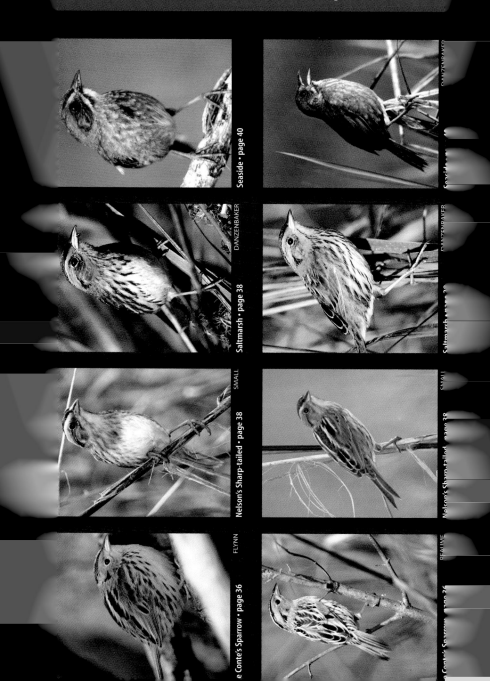

Seaside • page 40

DANZENBAKER

Saltmarsh • page 38

SMALL

Nelson's Sharp-tailed • page 38

FLYNN

e Conte's Sparrow • page 36

		Stripe		
Grasshopper	Buffy, no streaks	White	Buffy	Gray with fine rufous streaks
Henslow's	Buffy or whitish with dark streaks	Buffy or whitish with dark streaks	Olive	Olive with fine streaks
Le Conte's	Buffy-yellow with dark streaks	White	Buffy-yellow surrounding gray	Gray with fine rufous streaks
Nelson's Sharp-tailed	Buffy-orange with blurry streaks (throat buffy)	Gray	Buffy-orange surrounding gray	Plain gray
Saltmarsh Sharp-tailed	Buffy with dark streaks (throat white)	Gray	Buffy-orange surrounding gray	Plain gray
Seaside	Buffy-gray with dark streaks (throat white)	Gray	Mostly dark gray face with yellow lores	Plain gray

Henslow's Sparrow • page 34

FLYNN

rasshopper Sparrow • page 32

MCCAW

SMALL

Male Blue Grosbeak (first summer) · page 70

SMALL

Male Indigo Bunting (first spring) · page 72

FLYNN

Male Blue Grosbeak · page 70

REAUME

Male Indigo Bunting · page 72

SMALL

Female Blue Grosbeak · page 70

SMALL

Female Indigo Bunting · page 72

Blue Grosbeak / Indigo Bunting Chart

	Throat	Breast	Wings	Beak	Face	Head size
Blue Grosbeak	Female has light throat	Female usually has no streaks	Male has chestnut shoulder; female has light chestnut shoulder	Large and heavy	Male has black all around base of beak	Large- looking for body
Indigo Bunting	Female has whitish throat	Female usually has faint, blurry streaks	Male has no wingbars; first spring male may have slight wingbars; female has no or indistinct wingbars	Smaller	Male has black lores only	More proportional

FLYNN

Male House Finch • page 80

FLYNN

Female House Finch • page 80

MCCAW

Male Purple Finch • page 78

MCCAW

Female Purple Finch • page 78

Purple Finch / House Finch Comparison Chart

	Male color	Male color location	Male underpart markings	Female head pattern	Female underpart markings
Purple Finch	Raspberry or wine red	Fairly evenly distributed overall	Faint or distinct streaks on flanks	Whitish eyebrow	White with distinctive dark streaks
House Finch	Usually brick or fire-engine red	Distinct only on breast, forehead, eyebrow and rump	Brown streaks on sides, upper belly and undertail coverts	Quite plain	Grayish-brown with blurry streaks

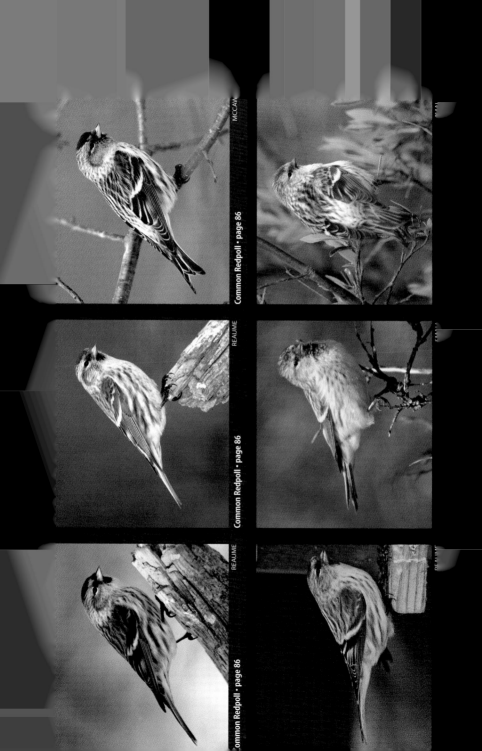

Common Redpoll • page 86

REAUME

Common Redpoll • page 86

REAUME

Common Redpoll • page 86

Redpoll Comparison Chart

	Size	Beak	Undertail coverts	Lower back (where wing meets back	Overall look	Breast & rump of adult male	Rump	Streaks on flanks
Common Redpoll	Same size or smaller	Finch-like	Usually streaked, only one or two in some males	Brownish	Brownish	Usually pink or reddish may have plain centre	Usually heavily streaked but may have plain centre	Usually thick & dark
Hoary Redpoll	Same size or bigger	Usually shorter-looking, gives face a "pushed-in" look	Usually unstreaked or up to three very thin streaks	Often a band of pale or whitish feathers	Frostier or whiter looking	Usually pale pink	Entire rump lightly streaked or unstreaked	Thin or faint streaks, though some females are heavily streaked

Note: These are very difficult to tell apart, and not all can be identified to species. Females of both species tend to be darker overall and more heavily streaked than males. "Greater" or "Greenland" Common Redpolls (subspecies *rostrata*) tend to be larger and darker overall than the "Southern" Common Redpoll (subspecies *flammea*) described and pictured here. "Hornemann's" Hoary Redpoll (subspecies *hornemanni*) tend to be larger and whiter than the "Southern" Hoary Redpoll (subspecies *exilipes*).

FLYNN

Lapland Longspur • page 62

FAIRBAIRN

Savannah Sparrow • page 30

REAUME

Hoary Redpoll • page 88

SMALL

Smith's Longspur • page 60

FLYNN

Vesper Sparrow • page 26

REAUME

Song Sparrow • page 44

FLYNN

Lincoln's Sparrow • page 46

MCCAW

Fox Sparrow • page 42

Streaked Underparts

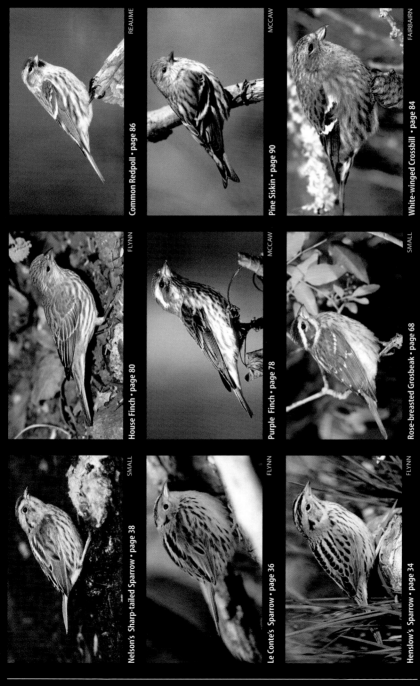

REAUME

Common Redpoll • page 86

MCCAW

Pine Siskin • page 90

FAIRBAIRN

White-winged Crossbill • page 84

FLYNN

House Finch • page 80

MCCAW

Purple Finch • page 78

SMALL

Rose-breasted Grosbeak • page 68

SMALL

Nelson's Sharp-tailed Sparrow • page 38

FLYNN

Le Conte's Sparrow • page 36

FLYNN

Henslow's Sparrow • page 34

Clay-colored Sparrow · page 22 — FLYNN

Chipping Sparrow · page 20 — REAUME

American Tree Sparrow · page 18 — REAUME

White-crowned Sparrow · page 54 — MCCAW

Field Sparrow · page 24 — FLYNN

Swamp Sparrow · page 48 — MCCAW

White-throated Sparrow · page 50 — MCCAW

Harris's Sparrow · page 52 — RICHARDS

Unstreaked or Faintly Streaked Underparts

American Goldfinch • page 92

Evening Grosbeak • page 94 — MCCAW

Dickcissel • page 74 — SMALL

Snow Bunting • page 64 — FLYNN

Red Crossbill • page 82 — MCCAW

Pine Grosbeak • page 76 — SMALL

Grasshopper Sparrow • page 32 — MCCAW

House Sparrow • page 96 — MCCAW

Indigo Bunting • page 72 — SMALL

Author's notes

To Dr. Sandy Middleton and our summers studying Chipping Sparrows and American Goldfinches. Thanks for your friendship, guidance and all those chocolate milkshakes!

Special thanks to Lea Martell for making this happen. I would like to also thank Karl Konze, Ron Lohr and Michelle Goodwin for reviewing earlier drafts. Thanks also go to Rob O. McAleer and Gareth B. Lind for their commitment, creativity and humour throughout the making of this book.

This book would not have been possible without the talent, generosity and patience of the photographers.

– Chris Earley

The range maps throughout the book were generously provided by: WILDSPACE™ 2002. WILDSPACE™ : digital hemispheric range maps for the breeding birds of Canada. Canadian Wildlife Service, Ontario Region, Ottawa, Ontario, Canada.

Credits

Photographers: Mike Danzenbaker, Scott Fairbairn, Jim Flynn, Robert McCaw, John Reaume, Jim Richards Brian E. Small, Doug Wechsler / Maxx Images/Animals Animals